Ocean Friends

SEA TURTLES

Dennis Rudenko

PowerKiDS press.
New York

Published in 2016 by The Rosen Publishing Group, Inc.
29 East 21st Street, New York, NY 10010

First Edition

Editor: Caitie McAneney
Book Design: Katelyn Heinle

Photo Credits: Cover, p. 1 Richard Whitcombe/Shutterstock.com; cover (series logo coral vector design) Koryaba/Shutterstock.com; back cover mycteria/Shutterstock.com; pp. 3–24 (interior coral vector design) etraveler/Shutterstock.com; p. 5 serg_dibrova/Shutterstock.com; pp. 6, 24 (coral reef) Khoroshunova Olga/Shutterstock.com; pp. 9, 24 (flipper) Kjeld Friis/Shutterstock.com; p. 10 Rich Carey/Shutterstock.com; pp. 13, 24 (seaweed) James A Dawson/Shutterstock.com; p. 14 (main) David Evison/Shutterstock.com; p. 14 (inset) antpkr/Shutterstock.com; p. 17 IrinaK/Shutterstock.com; p. 18 David Carbo/Shutterstock.com; p. 21 Brian J. Skerry/National Geographic Magazines/Getty Images; p. 22 Polly Dawson/Shutterstock.com.

Library of Congress Cataloging-in-Publication Data

Rudenko, Dennis, author.
Sea turtles / Dennis Rudenko.
pages cm. — (Ocean friends)
Includes index.
ISBN 978-1-5081-4185-3 (pbk.)
ISBN 978-1-5081-4186-0 (6 pack)
ISBN 978-1-5081-4187-7 (library binding)
1. Sea turtles—Juvenile literature. I. Title.
QL666.C536R83 2016
597.92'8—dc23

2015023510

Manufactured in the United States of America

CPSIA Compliance Information: Batch #BW16PK: For Further Information contact Rosen Publishing, New York, New York at 1-800-237-9932

CONTENTS

Sea turtles live in oceans all over the world.

Some sea turtles live in **coral reefs**. Coral reefs have many colorful plants and animals.

Most sea turtles have hard shells. They have **flippers** to help them swim.

shell
flippers

Sea turtles swim a long way to find food and a place to nest.

Sea turtles eat sea plants like **seaweed**. They also eat fish.

eggs

A mother sea turtle lays hundreds of eggs in holes on the beach.

Baby sea turtles break out of their eggs. They make their way to the ocean.

There are seven kinds of sea turtles. Green sea turtles have green and brown shells.

Leatherback turtles are the largest turtles in the world.

Sea turtles are cool ocean animals. Some can live to be over 50 years old!

WORDS TO KNOW

coral reef

flipper

seaweed

INDEX

WEBSITES

Due to the changing nature of Internet links, PowerKids Press has developed an online list of websites related to the subject of this book. This site is updated regularly. Please use this link to access the list: www.powerkidslinks.com/ocea/seat